quiet like a flame

Dedicated to
David & Cindy Danielson
for naming their daughter Faith and having faith
in her as a writer.

Dedicated to
Estera Baros
for continually believing in and championing
her daughter as an artist.

quiet like a flame

a collection of poems, prayers, and praise

Through Jesus, therefore, let us continually offer to God a sacrifice of praise - the fruit of lips that confess his name. And do not forget to do good and to share with others, for with such sacrifices is God pleased.
Hebrews 13:15-16 NIV

Sacrifice thank offerings to God,
fulfill your vows to the Most High,
and call upon me in the day of trouble;
I will deliver you, and you will honor me.
Psalm 50:14-15 NIV

Shout for joy to the Lord, all the earth.
Worship the Lord with gladness;
come before him with joyful songs.
Know that the Lord is God.
It is he who made us, and we are his;
we are his people, the sheep of his pasture.

Enter his gates with thanksgiving
and his courts with praise;
give thanks to him and praise his name.
For the Lord is good and his love endures forever;
his faithfulness continues through all generations.
Psalm 100 NIV

Be Still My Soul

Be still my soul, and praise Him.
Be still my soul, and be attentive to His word.
Surrender your restless anxiety;
Surrender your busy thoughts and plans.
Be obedient in rest, the Lord is won.
Sing praises, He is worthy.
Sing praises, He is good.
Sing praises, He is with us.
Sing praises, He is love.

A Prayer for Today

Peace in our places of labor,
Peace in our places of rest,
Confidence in the One who sustains us,
Assurance He will do what He says,
All tenderness and humility,
All joy and steadfast hope,
That we may look ever more like the Son
Through the power of the Spirit
And in unity with Love.

May Our Hearts Be Gracious

May our hearts be gracious
May our souls be sweet
Oh may we meet
One another in peace and humility

We Call You Abba

We call you Abba
Because you say you're Abba
Like a doting mama bird
You gather us close
Into your softest feathers
Your love sheds us of our fetters
That's who you are, my Abba
That's how you shelter me

We call you Yeshua
Because you show you're Yeshua
You are the branch
Under which we all gather
You call all the nations home
You are the Messiah
You set every captive free
My Yeshua, that's how you fight for me

We call you Ruach
Because you are Ruach Elohim
Gentle laugh in the stillness
You are the breath in me
Your wind lights a fire
That burns bright for liberty
Yes you are holy fire
Ruach ever refining me

Speak of the Coming King

Speak of the coming King
Speak of the King of Peace
Speak of the mustard seed
Seek out the Holy of holies

He will be found by those who seek
He will be found as joy complete
He will be found on the mercy seat
The faithful One who intercedes

Be known by Him, He is worthy
Be known by Him, He redeems
Be known by Him, the Shepherd-King
Who calls to you with a love song

Hear Him, beloved, keep watch
Seek Him, beloved, fear not
Beloved, be known and grown by His love
He is the coming King, He is the King of Peace

Remain in You

what grace that I was never meant to be
enough for this,
that the call has never been to descend alone
into the ache of the world,
no, you have always gone before me into pain,
always been present with me in suffering,
ever on the other side of the struggle and in
the midst of it holding peace and rest
yes, I will rest in you,
with
d e e p
s l o w
breaths
I will rest in you,
will abide and remain attached to you, the vine,
the sweetest wine, the daily bread sustaining,
from your depths of wisdom I draw strength,
from the wells of your comfort and grace,
you are life, you are the wellspring,
you are always offering communion with
yourself to me,
always welcoming me in weariness,
taking the burdens off my shoulders,
the weight off my chest that presses so,
and covering me with your robe,
yoking my heart to yours and thereby giving
me lightness, rest, peace, the deep humming
joy of you.

Your Glory Overflows

You go before me
You are breath inside me
You withhold no good thing
For You are the greatest
And Your glory overflows

Father, fill me
Overfull with Your glory
Let my life pour out
For You are the greatest
And Your glory overflows

For You are the greatest
And Your glory overflows

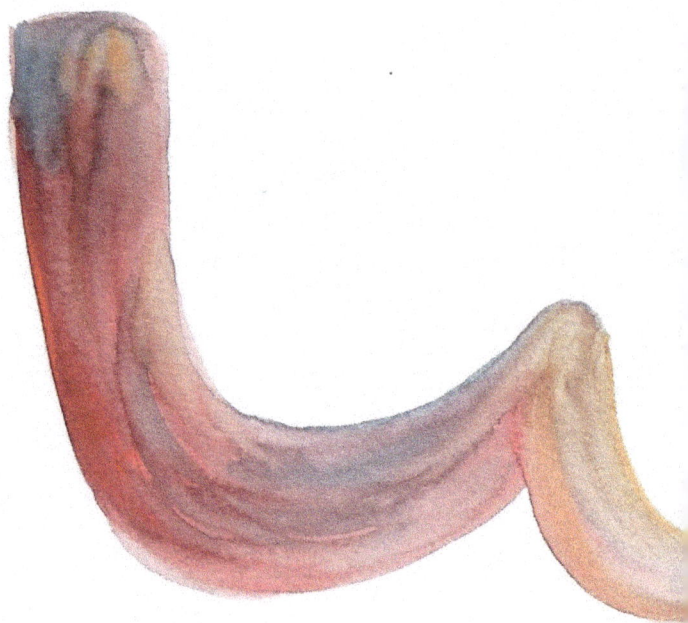

All the Colors of Your Majesty

We stand in all the colors of Your majesty,
In awe and completely amazed.
There is a nail-pierced hand on our hearts,
A voice speaking, "Known. Loved. Forgiven. Redeemed."
And all the colors of Your majesty dance,
They sing and shout with praise, "You are holy."

Prayer

A sacrifice of praise
A lament
Where my lack – of wisdom, hope, strength –
Meets Your all-sufficiency
A deep breath and loosening of shoulders
A movement
A surrendered tongue
Holy tears
A scream
A shout
An honest whimper

Lord, make me like You.
Create in me a clean heart, O God,
Renew a steadfast spirit within me
That I may meet You, every day,
And be changed.

Sufficient in My Insufficiency

It's you, Jesus,
Sufficient in my insufficiency.
It's you, Jesus,
Righteousness and holiness in me.
It's you, Jesus,
My Jesus,
My King.

Only you
Meet me in my brokenness
Without an ounce of shame,
You give me your wholeness,
You give me a name.

I am found in you,
In the sparkle of your eye,
In the scarred skin on your side,
I am found in you,
My Jesus,
My King.

Lord, take all of me,
I give you my yes,
Surrender to your rest
And your refining light.

My Jesus, my King, take all of me,
So we may be one as you are one,
Make me fully in the image of the Son.

Sweetest Shepherd of Joy

I can tell no story by my own, and its substance
is yoked to my honesty: If I will be frank and let
my words uncover me, then I will be found truly,
simply, humbly.

One night I asked, "Lord, what would you have
me surrender? What am I holding to so tightly
that You are not what I cling to directly?"
He answered, "Significance."

Oooof. Wanting so much to be something
worthwhile, someone remembered for good words
and deeds, revered as one with high integrity,
dear meekness, great joy.

Significance. There is a greater glory. I need not
strive to be seen. It is in the day to day, hour by
hour, minute by minute humdrum that You want
to be found by me.

The need for grand gestures was satisfied on the
cross. And when the stone rolled away and You
walked. And when the Spirit came to dwell in me
as a temple of the Living God.

Performance is worth so much less than intimacy.
When I let myself be known by You in heartbreak,
in my deep ache for fullness and closeness, I find
You true as Comforter.

When You gently pick apart my pride with its gross lie of self-sufficiency, and when You shush my murmuring shame so that I can hear myself honestly, I find You real as Counselor.

When You listen to my grief and frustration and confusion about the world and Your bride and show me in turn Your great grief and compassion, I find You as the Carpenter and as the Man of Sorrows.

Elyssa Faith. Elicit faith, to call it forth, cosmos in the chaos, clearness in the melee, sincere belief despite the darkness. You saw fit that I carry this name and told me to walk in gentleness.

Elyssa: God is my oath. My portion. My daily bread. My firm foundation. My King. The One who sits with me, spurs me on, sasses me, creates so beautifully in this life and in eternity.

Jesus, I will look to You, my dear Aslan on the move, as the young at heart are wont to do, for I know You are faithful to be found when I seek You with sincerity.

Dear Bridegroom, I surrender my search for significance. Surrender it all to You who are peace in the quiet moments and in the overwhelming noise. Thanks for being with me here, before, now, forever, Sweetest Shepherd of Joy.

The Sweetness of Rest

help me to honor
every soul that I see
with the sweetness of rest
that You have given to me

You Sit Close and Quiet with Me

You sit close and quiet with me,
Calm and unafraid of intimacy.
There is no fear in the love you lavish on me,
No pressure to perform in just the right way.
You are the gardener-king;
Firmly and gently pruning,
Revealing the bitter fruits and their source uprooting.
Your tenderness is my portion, your gentleness,
Your compassionate love, there is much to you,
But to me you give tenderness,
So I will take hold of your sweetness,
Will welcome your fragrance,
Will stay here in your gaze.
Lord, I need your tender boldness.
Lord, I need your wisdom and grace.

Humble As Clay

Be dearly soft and tender
Submit to leading like a lamb
Be fully meek and humble
Submit to bleeding like the Lamb

Be boldly gracious and loving
Move with passion like a lion
Be wholly generous and steady
Move with compassion like the Lion

Be all things to all people
That they may know Him
Who was and is and is to come
That they may see Him
Through your weakness
Through the roar you roar by His strength
Be made like Him
Be humble as clay

Work in Me

Work in me Your gentleness
Work in me Your peace
Work in me Your righteousness
I'll just sit here at Your feet

Stretch me in humility
Help me ever seek Your face
For all You want to grow in me
Oh to rest in Your sweet gaze

Lord, I trust Your sovereignty
Lord, I trust Your grace
I surrender everything
To the wonder of Your ways

You Are Love Unrelenting

You are love unrelenting
Calling me deeper into the mystery of you

In the chaos, you are stillness
In the heartbreak, you grieve
In all that I don't understand
You move and lead in sovereignty

You are love unrelenting
Calling me deeper into the mystery of you
You are peace surely mending
Calling me deeper into the grace of all you do

I won't run from you: I'll stay close and learning
I won't run from you: I'll dwell in your tender mercy

Tender-hearted worship
breaks the will and force of the enemy.
Sovereign love and peace
shatter the power of sin.

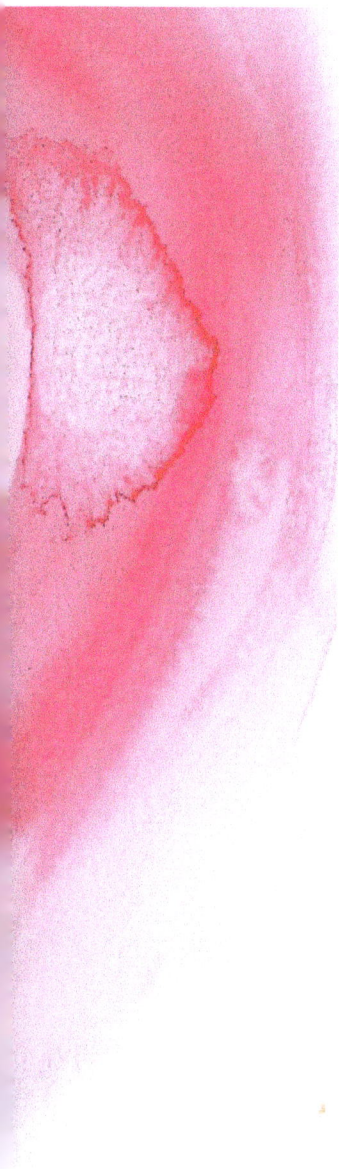

Tender-Hearted Worship

Faithful to All, Faithful to Each

Faithful to all and faithful to each
Faithful to all and faithful to each

Go, tell of it
Stand on it
Dwell in it

He is faithful to all and faithful to each
He is faithful to all and faithful to each

Go, tell of it
Stand on it
Dwell in it

Pause

Pause to rest and reorient
To recognize and remember
The one thing worthy of worship

Pause and do not rush to restart
Realignment takes dear time
There is much to adjust and resettle

Pause and return to your wonder
Reclaim childlike certainty in the waymaker
In the Spirit who hovered over the waters
And who came as fire to waken hearts to life

Pause to then run with renewed purpose
Restored hope and revitalized vision
Toward and alongside the one who sees you
And calls you to wholeness in him

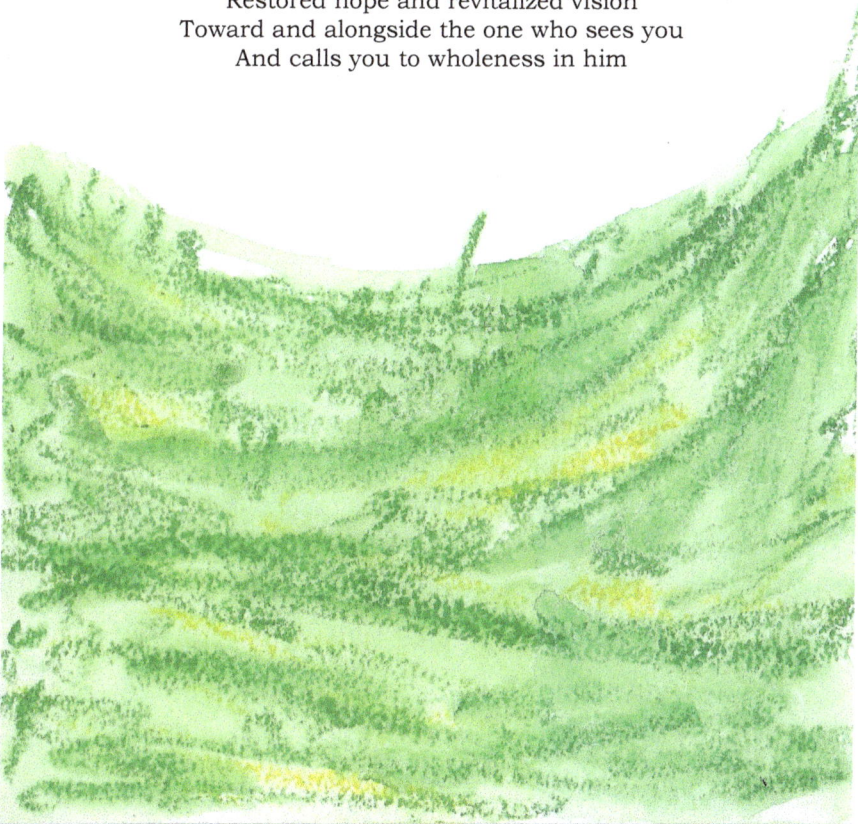

God's Love

God's love is not hollow, brittle, or less substantial than it seems.
God's love is fullness, the core and foundation of being.

God's love is not fickle, capricious, or subject to moods that swing.
God's love is constant, beyond time, and just in judgment and mercy.

God's love is not vague, incomplete, or uncertain of its plans.
God's love is specific, absolute, and faithful to its purposes.

God's love speaks, dances, and sings.
God's love heals, laughs, and redeems.
God's love is the truth and rightness of things.

Rest in Time

For your mind, dynamic and formidable,
Rest in time, create space to be empty.

For your body, soft and weather-worn,
Rest in time, create space to be held.

For your heart, passionate and growing,
Rest in time, create space to be light.

For your soul, vibrant and searching,
Rest in time, create space to be found.

For your dear self, every component and part,
Your dear self is loved and made to love,
Forgiven and made to forgive,
Created and made to create,
Delighted in and made for delight.

And your dear self, all of you, is formed to move
In tandem, in some sweet, miraculous unity,
With family, the bride, the body, as one.
Rest in time, be made whole, pause, grieve, and laugh:
There is so much life in rest.

Father of Kindness

Father of kindness
Father of peace
Father of kindness
I'll stay here at the seat
Of the table you set for me
I'll stay here and I'll feast
In the presence of my enemies
I'll dance on disappointment
Laugh at insecurities
Spirit within me
Spirit upon me
Christ before me
The blood and the wine
Oh Father, you are so kind
So I'll stay, I'll stay, I'll stay
I'll stay at the seat of the table
You set for me

Oh Jesus, it's only ever been you
Oh Jesus, it's only ever been you
You're the only one who saves

You and Only You

With you I can move gracefully
With you I can be freely seen
Through you and only you is my bare heart
Made beautiful, made clean, sent out rejoicing

Tear stains shine like gold in your covering
Tender scars hold no shame in your midst
Through you and only you is my raw pain
Given dignity, given grace, brought to restoration

You and only you
My king upon that cross
Dear friend of Lazarus
Child about your Father's business
You and only you are life and love abundant

Peace and Still More Peace

My prayer for those I love
Is peace and still more peace.
Peace to your body,
That you may let tension move through
And then be released, so that you may rest.
Peace to your mind,
That grief may be recognized and given time,
That anxiety may be met with grace,
That spiraling thoughts may swirl to a stop
And be brought back down into proportion.
Peace to your heart,
That shame may be washed gently away
That you may know and accept forgiveness,
That the embers of hopeful joy still simmering,
Still warm after all this time, would be seen
And met with kindness, tenderness, life,
That your heart may ignite into a steady flame,
A steady flame of peace.

Spirit, would you speak through me?

And when I cannot find the words,
Spirit, would you speak through me?
I trust your words burn righteously on my tongue,
I trust that you edify, purify, and comfort,
I trust your presence in me is honoring,
That you are making me more like yourself,
More fully in tune with the heart of Love,
As we partner together in prayer, Spirit,
Holy Spirit, run over, overflow, be glorified
On earth as you are in heaven,
Let heaven come and spill forth from me
Continuously, without ceasing,
Let me be a living sacrifice of praise
To you, for you, through you, with you
Always always always always

You seek me out and call me forth

into Your splendor, into Your court of worship.

You Seek Me Out and Call Me Forth

Fountain of Truth

You are the fountain of truth overflowing
Bursting up and out into creation
Gushing and rushing to fill every empty place

You restore the broken-hearted
You restore the broken-hearted
You restore the broken-hearted
That's who You are
That's just who You are

It's All for You

It's all for You.
All of these tears,
All this surrender,
It's all for You
And You're more than worthy of it all.
You're more than worthy of it all.
Jesus, You're more than worthy of it all.

Jesus, You snatched me up and You haven't let me go.
You've held me close when I thought I was unlovable.
You've poured out rest upon me, so that I can sing
With true gladness in my heart, all of my days.
So all of my days, I'll give all of me for Your glory.

Father Who Sees Me

Father You have come
To my broken heart You run
You pick me up
You spin me 'round
Your love abounds

Father You are here
My anxious thoughts You steer
Back to You
Back to You
Always back to You

You love so freely
Father who sees me
You love so freely
Father who sees me

Testimony

Testimony
It is not a hidden thing
It is the name I carry
It is my bare face open to you
Testimony is deep light
Working out from within and dancing
Rejoicing and weaving into every fiber of my being

I have been redeemed

Heaviness still comes and grief
In the midst of everything
Every joy and prayer and breath and meal
I am known and I am not alone
I am held and dwelt with
Oh ever-present grace

Father of Rest

Take this heaviness and make it sweet,
Show us all of Your tender mercy,
We come in weariness to sit at Your feet,
Father of Rest, meet us in our weeping
That we may grieve with You,
Surrounded by Your promise
That all love is found in You.

Here Is My Heart

Here is my heart
Out in the open
Fully exposed
And safe

My heart is safe here
I can't begin to understand it
My heart is safe here with you
I will not be abandoned
My heart is safe here with you
I can't begin to understand it
My heart is safe here

Lay It All Down Again

Lay it all down again, every single day.
Lay it all down again, your need to be affirmed and praised.
Lay it all down again, let Him put His yoke upon you,
God who came as man,
God who served and washed your hands and feet.
Lay it all down again. He alone is worthy.
Jesus is worthy of it all.

Simple Yes

I give You my simple yes
Every day anew
I give You my helplessness
You will see me through

You are patient oh so kind
You are steady too
You dissolve the lies that bind
You hold all that's true

I give You my simple yes
Every day anew
Form in me Your righteousness
That I may look like You

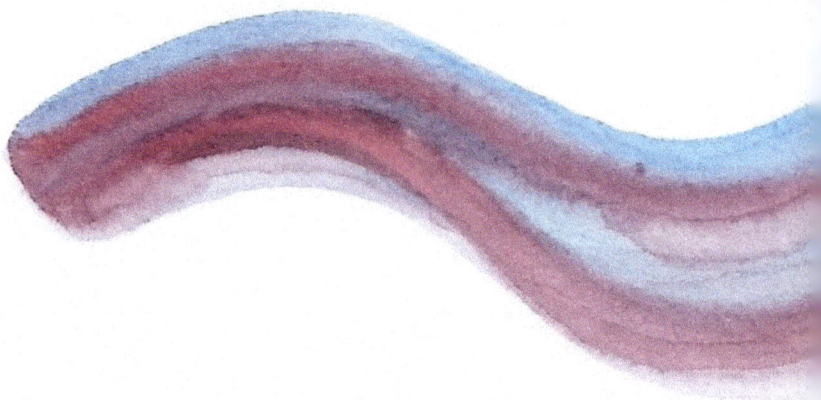

Let humility
Keep you low
In worship

The King is coming
Let what is dead stay dead
Let the old man fall away

Feel His feet hit the ground
Hear His song
Lift your eyes to see
His coming

RISE

As the Spirit prepares
Your heart for the King

Fall

In the River of Your Love

In the river of Your love,
In the light of Your presence,
I will worship You,
For You are my soul's delight,
You who are holy and wholly good.

Here Steadily Are You

With each fresh day may my prayer be: Here I am.
In my weakness and in Your strength: Here I am.

You know my need for rest, for stretching,
You measure grace enough for me to say: Here I am.

Here I am. Here steadily are You.

SEE

See clearly into the heart of God,
It is open to you.
See the Trinity healing the broken-hearted
And binding up your wounds with patience
And gentleness and wholeness and truth.
Oh see the sweetest love, the most profound,
The most humble, the most mighty.

See the Spirit of resurrection life
Running towards you with arms wide open,
Speaking truth to lies and shattering chains
Of death and deception. Be known
By the truth and let the truth set you free.

See the Kingdom of God is coming and present here.
See the King of joy and laughter,
See the angels and saints dancing alongside Him,
His fully redeemed bride rejoicing
In the triumphant love of the King,
The One who speaks hope into reality,
Into existence, with full authority.

See the One who is worthy and worship
At His throne.
Emmanuel. Yeshua. Yahweh.
King of kings. Holy One.

Worth Waiting Up For

You said, "together forever, you and me, together forever, shamelessly."
You're worth waiting up for, you my King, you are worth everything.

The fire on the altar must be kept burning; it must not go out. Every morning the priest is to add firewood and arrange the burnt offering on the fire and burn the fat of the fellowship offerings on it. The fire must be kept burning on the altar continuously; it must not go out.
Leviticus 6:12-13 NIV

Be dressed and ready for service and keep your lamps burning, like men waiting for their master to return from a wedding banquet, so that when he comes and knocks they can immediately open the door for him.
Luke 12:35-36 NIV

Fasten me upon your heart as a seal
of fire forevermore.
This living, consuming flame
will seal you as my prisoner of love.
My passion is stronger
than the chains of death and the grave,
all consuming as the very flashes of fire
from the burning heart of God.
Place this fierce, unrelenting fire
over your entire being.
Rivers of pain and persecution
will never extinguish this flame.
Endless floods will be unable
to quench this raging fire that burns within you.
Everything will be consumed.
It will stop at nothing
as you yield everything to this furious fire
until it won't even seem to you like a sacrifice anymore.
Song of Songs 8:6-7 TPT

About the artist
Kayla Baros is a Central Texas based artist with a global mindset and heart set on stewarding creativity to co-create with and bring glory to our Creator. She is a founder and leader of Acts Church Creatives, an interdisciplinary ministry in Waco, Texas.

instagram: @kaylabaros & @actschurchcreatives

About the author
Elyssa Faith Danielson loves to simply bring praise to the Lord and quite often this spills out in poetry. In publishing this book, she prays the Holy Spirit moves through the pages to readers like a balm, bringing comfort, rest, hope, and life - the real, deep kinds that were paid for in full by the blood of Jesus Christ.

instagram: @elyssafaith
spotify: faith danielson > quiet like a flame

www.ingramcontent.com/pod-product-compliance
Lightning Source LLC
Chambersburg PA
CBHW041823090426
42811CB00010B/1088